Eric Wood Centers on What's Good

Featuring Eric Wood

From the Creators of

"There's Always a Way with Stevie J!"
"Freddy J Makes His Play"
"The Legend of FitzMagic Mr. Nomadic"

Written by Charles Roberts III and Stevie Johnson
Illustrated by Zachary McCabe

Cover photo of Eric Wood by Jeffrey T. Barnes
www.jeffreytbarnesphotography.com

With support from ImagineWe Publishers
www.imaginewepublishers.com

ISBN: 979-8-218-52157-8 (Paperback)
ISBN: 979-8-218-52158-5 (Hardback)

First Edition

TO ALL OF OUR READERS:
MAY YOU DARE TO DREAM BIG
- AND HAVE THE COURAGE
TO LIVE YOUR DREAMS.

Visit our website today! https://hbhf-creators.com

Sometimes, the people who do the hardest work don't get the glory. But for Eric Wood, it's a much different story.

Eric played professional football on the team's offensive line. He didn't get to score touchdowns, and for him – that was just fine.

Eric took pride in his role on Buffalo's team. As the center, he snapped the ball to the quarterback and was living his dream.

If Eric did his job well, the announcers would rarely mention him by name. But his teammates knew Eric was one of the most important players in the game.

When the quarterback stayed upright and the running back had space to run, it made everything much more fun.

Eric has always believed everyone should share in the joy.
Because being part of a team is not just about one girl or boy.

It's very hard to succeed when you don't look out for one another. This is a lesson Eric learned early in life from Evan, his younger brother.

Evan could not walk or talk, but he smiled as bright as a star. His positivity motivated Eric to cherish life and work hard to go far.

When Eric felt down or out, he thought
of Evan and everything he went through.
With Evan's smile in mind, Eric had support, too.

It helped Eric through some of his worst days. Football is a physical sport, and he got hurt many times and many ways.

In fact, the doctor gave Eric some bad news during his first professional year. He had two broken bones in his leg – which was exactly what he did not want to hear.

And just two years later, Eric injured his knee.
How could this be?

The head coach encouraged Eric to let it go and not get too mad. Eric reminded himself to think of Evan and how he smiled when others in his position probably would be sad.

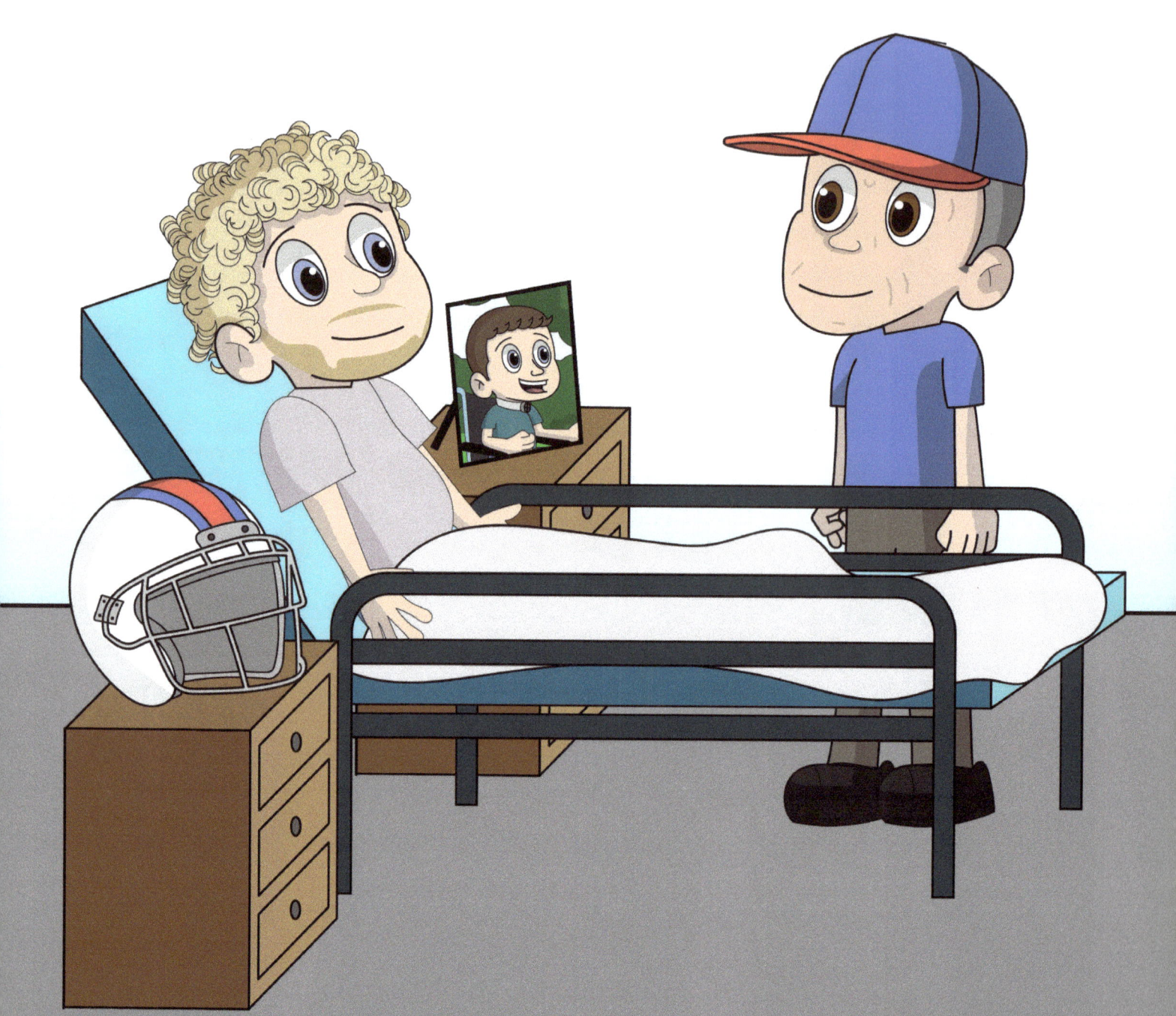

As his injuries healed throughout his career, Eric enjoyed ime with the most important people in his life – friends and family, especially his always-supportive wife.

When he got back on the field, he had no reason to frown. Just like teammates such at Stevie Johnson, Fred Jackson and Ryan Fitzpatrick – he was a fan-favorite in this town.

Eric and his teammates loved hearing the crowd roar.
The fans stuck by their side, no matter the score.

One of his favorite moments was becoming captain of that team in Buffalo. But as a locker-room leader, he had many larger goals to go.

Next, he'd play in the Pro Bowl, which is football's all-star game. But what he really wanted was to bring Buffalo back to playoff fame.

Eric was a part of the Buffalo team that made the playoffs for the first time in 17 long years. Fans and players alike enjoyed the clinching moment with celebratory tears.

Everyone watched the final minute between Cincinnati and Baltimore – and jumped for joy when there was a game-winning score!

When Cincinnati won, it meant Buffalo earned a playoff spot. Finally, Eric and his teammates had a shot.

Although that first playoff game didn't quite go their way, the Buffalo team learned from the moment and held its head high the very next day.

Due to one more injury, the playoff game was Eric's last as a pro. Today, he's one of the team's radio broadcasters – and thrilled to still be part of the show.

There's one more thing he wants you to hear:
When things get tough, always remember to remain
positive – and keep family and friends near!

Try to see if you can find all of the professional aliens featured in this book!

Football Player   Librarian   Coach   Baseball Player

President   Basketball Player   Superhero   Police Officer   Chef

Tennis Player   Architect   Barber   Golfer

About the HBHF Creators

About Author Stevie Johnson (AKA "Stevie J. Styles")

Stevie, who lives by the mantra "Handle Biz, Have Fun," is a former professional football player for the Buffalo Bills, San Francisco 49ers, and San Diego Chargers. He was the first player in Bills history to post back-to-back seasons of 1,000 receiving yards or more – and even added a third straight year for good measure. Today, Stevie and his family reside in San Diego. He founded and continues to manage the ClubHBHF and Exposure Academy, which are geared toward educating up-and-coming football players and providing a platform to display talent.

About Author Charles Roberts III (AKA "CR3")

Charles, who goes by Charlie, is a former sportswriter who now works in public relations by day and writes books after the sun sets. He earned a bachelor's degree in journalism at Buffalo State College and spends his free time running, creating content and enjoying every moment of raising his daughter, Zoey. Charlie and his wife, April, have Zoey and a rambunctious dog named Layla.

About Illustrator Zachary McCabe (AKA "Run ZMC")

Zachary, who goes by Zack, is an architecture professional who spends his free time painting, creating art and – of course – illustrating. Zack, a diehard Buffalo sports fan and frequent golfer, earned both his Bachelor of Science and Masters in Architecture at the University at Buffalo. He and his wife, Kelly, live in Buffalo with their daughter, Sophia, and their dog, Cali.